G000123551

TO

Ann

FROM

Happy
Birthday!

DATE

Written by Sarah B. Chaplin
Illustration and design by Melanie Chadwick Copyright © 2021
Printed by Kingdom Print, Cornwall www.kingdomprint.org.uk
Published by Truth Told

All scripture quotations unless otherwise stated are taken from the Holy Bible, New International Version
©1973, 1978, 1984, 2011 by International Bible Society. Used by permission. All rights reserved.

Copyright © 2021 Sarah Chaplin - Truth Told
Foreword Copyright © 2021 Tamie Downes
All rights reserved.

ISBN - 978-1-8381143-2-9

Inspirational / Encouragement / Women / Christian Life
To book Sarah please visit www.truthtold.org.uk
To commission Melanie please visit www.melaniechadwick.com

PEARLS FOR THE GIRLS

SARAH CHAPLIN

ILLUSTRATED BY MELANIE CHADWICK

To those who have encouraged us to communicate truth, be creative, and dedicate these gifts to God.

FOREWORD

Sarah and I first met in 2006 when my husband was speaking at her church in Porthleven. We had both recently moved to the small fishing village, and were both the wives of Church Ministers. I remember being awe-struck by her ability to play the piano so beautifully with only one hand (Sarah was born with only one arm). I soon realised this was a tiny part of her incredible God given skills as an inspirational speaker, writer, hospital chaplain and of course mother to four gorgeous children. At the end of the service I introduced myself and there was an instant connection between us. We became firm friends, meeting as often as we could for coffee and cake and rejuvenating time together.

I am delighted to commend this book to you. In it, you too will get to meet the real Sarah. She writes as she is, full of honesty and humour. I have been trying to encourage Sarah to put it together since I first read one of her 'Pearls for the Girls' flyers many years ago. It seemed obvious to me that her pearls of wisdom needed to be shared with others, not just in her community, or around the country, but in a far broader way. It is also clear that this book will be useful in many different contexts. It has proved its worth in the original target audience of young mums, however I am sure it will also be an encouragement to women of all ages, or to be given as a thought provoking gift to friends and family.

Sarah is an amazing woman, full of rich wisdom and abundant love for others. She has an incredible gift of communicating, which is demonstrated in these pages. The original 'pearls' have not only brightened the days of many mums, but often been taken home to be pinned on fridges and read by husbands and grandmas and anyone else passing through the homes of Porthleven! Their impact has been huge - with many stories of lives being helped, encouraged and challenged by these inspirational words.

In the business of modern society it is easy to pass over opportunities to read. A parable in the Bible tells us that a pearl of great price is worth making sacrifices for. The treasures within these pages are easy to read, and full of truth; you will be well rewarded for any time set aside reading them.

Dr Tamie Downes
March 2021

Dr Tamie Downes is a GP in Oxford and is married to Greg and has two beautiful daughters Anastasia and Trinity.

HELLO

Thank you so much for opening this book of ours!

On its pages we pour out our thoughts, observations and questions, about all sorts of topics from everyday situations and common feelings that we hope you can relate to.

These 'Pearls' are Bible-based thoughts about things learned, or are being learned on the journey, and ask you questions that will make you think, pause for thought and consider what is written, and how it applies to you and your life.

This is a book that you can dip in and out of and there should be something here for everyone of all ages.

Our main hope is that through sharing these stories, thoughts and artwork we are able to inspire and encourage you.

We hope and pray that you will find something for the situation you are in at just the right time, and that it will make a difference and give you hope.

SARAH & MEL

With Special thanks to...

We are both grateful for our husbands Glen and Tony, for their patience as we have worked on the production of this book. Both couples work as a team, and we are thankful for their ongoing love and support.

To Tamie Downes for the nudge to get this into print, and her encouragement in communicating truth to a wider audience.

To Helen Waring and Sally Berriman for proofreading, helping with editing and giving of their time and love to this publication.

We are both indebted to our family and friends who have been a part of our journey of faith through the years, and to those who have mentored us and prayed for us.

52 PEARLS

APPLES

The look on my young son's face as he bit into a bruised apple was one of horror. I quickly rectified the situation by removing all the 'brown', and he was happy. Somewhere between the supermarket and home damage had been done, and the poor apple had received an injury.

A bruise comes from a blow of some sort, and so just like the apple, we can also have bruises appear on our bodies and we may not recall exactly what caused it. More significant than a bruised arm or leg however is a bruised heart.

Sometimes things happen in life and we are on the receiving end of hurtful words or actions, and they can bruise us.

Bruises hurt and can often be tender for a long time after the initial injury. They leave their mark, whether on our bodies or in our heart.

What is the remedy? To forgive the offender or the one who wounded you is the very first step. It's easy to say, but not so easy to do, so start right now by asking God for help.

Pray for the person and ask for blessing on their lives.

You can choose to hold the pain, and let it spread and turn things sour, or let go of it, by starting to forgive.

BLESS
THOSE *WHO* PERSECUTE YOU

BLESS &
do *NOT*
curse
ROMANS 12:14

BEAUTY

What's the first thing that comes to mind when you think of the word beautiful? Is it a word that you'd use to describe yourself?

Is beauty something that only a few attain? Is it all about what you see? Or does real beauty come from within?

Outer beauty, and the many cosmetic products available, are making some companies a lot of money, but the beauty that exudes from inside you doesn't cost a penny.

Outer beauty can cause competition, jealousy, disappointment and rivalry, but inner beauty is all to do with your character, attitude and the condition of your heart.

The Bible calls it the 'inner beauty of the heart' and in God's eyes this inner beauty is of great worth to Him.

So are you beautiful? Do you feel beautiful? Remember it's not about how many times you are complimented or whether your hair and make-up is just right.

When the heart is beautiful, the face just has to display the evidence.

Next time you are quick to judge yourself in the mirror, stop, pause and think; what is beautiful in God's eyes?

YOUR BEAUTY SHOULD NOT COME FROM OUTWARD ADORNMENT, SUCH AS ELABORATE HAIRSTYLES GOLD JEWELLERY OR FINE CLOTHES. RATHER, IT SHOULD BE THAT OF YOUR INNER SELF THE UNFADING BEAUTY OF A GENTLE & QUIET SPIRIT, WHICH IS OF GREAT WORTH IN GOD'S SIGHT.

1 PETER 3:3-4

BLAME

When my husband and I lived in Wales and our children were young, one day unexpectedly, crayon marks appeared on our lounge wall. I made some general enquiries of our four children, and all of them totally denied it. I eventually lined the four of them up like an identity parade, confronting them one by one. Not only did they all deny it, but they also found great pleasure in blaming someone else in the family, and I never did get to solve that mystery.

In life, it is so easy to point the blame at others and blame others for something only you and I can take responsibility for. It is also possible that no one in particular is directly to blame for the situations in life we can't control.

When my Mum died of cancer in 2010, having been diagnosed a few weeks earlier, it was a terrible shock for us as a family.

Could this have been detected sooner? Is blame even an option here? Who's fault was it that it hadn't been found?

We had been told that it was a rare cancer, and almost impossible to detect, so we concluded that there was no need to play the 'blame game'. In the long run it would not benefit us at all, and would leave a bitter taste in our mouths.

We made a conscious decision to accept what had happened and with God's help, we had peace of mind as a result.

BE JOYFUL IN
HOPE
PATIENT IN
AFFLICTION
FAITHFUL IN
PRAYER

ROMANS 12:12

CHICKENS

We have had chickens for a number of years now, and it's lovely each morning collecting the freshly laid eggs. We regularly have chicks, and I love watching the hen look after her young. I'm reminded of this story:

"A young Nigerian boy named Olu had a pet chicken. They became great friends and inseparable companions. One day the hen disappeared and Olu cried and cried.

Then after three weeks the hen returned to the compound with seven beautiful chicks. The Nigerian boy was overjoyed and the mother took great care of her brood.

One day late in the dry season, the bush was set on fire, and when the fire was over, Olu and his friends walked through the smouldering embers. The boy noticed a heap of charred feathers. It looked like the remains of a bird that had not escaped from the fire.

Then Olu realized in horror that it was his beloved friend, the hen, all black and burned to death. But then came the sounds of chicks.

The mother hen had covered them with her body and they were still alive and well.

She had given her life for them so they may live."
From a story called 'Little Red Hen' K.S.Wakefield. 1945

The Bible says in Psalm 91:4 that God will 'cover us with His feathers, and under His wings you will find refuge.'

God is willing to protect and help us when things get too much to bear. All we need to do is hide in Him. Jesus 'laid down' His life for us so that we could live. That's true love.

He will cover you with his feathers and

Under his wings you will find refuge; his faithfulness will be your shield and rampart.

PSALM 91:4

CONQUERING FEAR

What causes you to curl up inside, or makes you want to run a mile? Spiders? Confined spaces? Thunder and lightning? The dentist? Your mother-in-law? Are there things that you are afraid of or scare you senseless? Would you attempt a rope bridge over a gorge? Or sky-diving? Or pot-holing?

We are all different, and what causes us to feel fear will be different too.

So what's the cure?

If you are going to a hospital appointment and feel a bit scared, you might ask a friend to go with you. Why? Because it's comforting and you feel less apprehensive.

In Psalm 23 it says 'The Lord is my shepherd', and continues to say 'I will fear no evil because You are with me'.

So many people in the Bible found amazing strength from hearing God's reassurance that He was with them, and that in itself made all the difference.

The Bible says love is the antidote, in that lovely verse 'Perfect love drives out fear' 1 John 4:18. Our fear also subsides when we know someone is right alongside us.

So are you facing a fearful situation right now? Ask God to be with you.

He is always the best antidote for fear.

SO DO NOT FEAR,
FOR I AM WITH YOU;
DO NOT BE DISMAYED,
FOR I AM YOUR GOD.

I WILL STRENGTHEN
YOU AND HELP YOU,
I WILL UPHOLD YOU
WITH MY RIGHTEOUS
RIGHT HAND.

ISAIAH 41:10

DISAPPOINTMENT

Have you ever been disappointed? It's generally other people that we get disappointed with, but sometimes we get disappointed with ourselves, and we can feel a failure for different reasons.

Disappointment is the emotion you feel when an expectation is not met.

When what we had hoped for doesn't work out, it may seem like the end of the world. But just because one thing didn't quite go the way you thought it might, it doesn't mean you are a failure, or that disappointment and failure will always be in your life. We learn a lot by going through disappointments.

Being able to talk about your disappointments with someone you trust, giving yourself time to recover, and letting your emotions out in a way that doesn't hurt others will all help ease the disappointment. It's important to share, as disappointment that is not dealt with can lead to depression. We can move on from the setback, and look for better days ahead.

One thing is certain, despite life's uncertainties, Jesus is not a disappointment. He won't let you down and there's not many people you can say that about.

And what's more, when you feel no one cares about the things in your life that disappoint you, He does.

NEVER

will I

LEAVE

you

NEVER

will I

FORSAKE

you.

HEBREWS 13:5

DON'T COMPARE

In the supermarket we often find ourselves comparing one product against another, whether on price, best value, taste or calories. If you remember back to your school days, some essay questions instructed you to 'compare and contrast' certain topics, and come to some conclusions.

In day-to-day life it's so easy to use comparison. We compare ourselves with each other, and compare our children with other children. For example you may not have taken your first steps until you were eighteen months old, whereas your friend was running a marathon by eleven months!

Don't compare. It comes with problems. It opens the door to feelings of inadequacy and jealousy, superiority and inferiority, and those feelings will do you no favours.

You are unique and fabulous just the way you are, and so are your precious children, if you have them. When you realise this and let it settle in your heart, whatever anyone else has or doesn't have, or is able to do or not do becomes less of an issue.

When tempted to compare, contrast and think all sorts of unhelpful thoughts, have a re-think.

WHOLE GRAIN

FRESH

HOT

STRONG MUSTARD

I PRAISE YOU
BECAUSE I AM
FEARFULLY &
WONDERFULLY
MADE; YOUR
WORKS ARE
WONDERFUL
I KNOW THAT
FULL WELL.

PSALM 139:14

DON'T BE AFRAID TO SAY NO

Have you ever found yourself saying 'yes' when you really wanted to say 'no'? For whatever reason, whether it was an invite to a function, or a request to do something that didn't quite fit in with your plans, you said 'yes', and then felt the stress kick in! Sometimes it's hard to say 'no', because you feel a certain obligation and you think that your 'no' will cause problems, or that you are rejecting that person, although this really isn't the case.

With parenting children, don't ever be afraid to say 'no' to them. You may feel bad when you say it, but it is for their own good, because 'no' is either protecting them, helping them, or teaching them right from wrong; therefore it is a good thing.

And don't think that the 'no' word has to wait until they are toddlers. Babies are pretty clever little people too, and they will benefit from learning the 'no' word nice and early on.

Matthew 5:37 says simply let your 'Yes' be 'Yes,' and your 'No,' 'No.' This encourages us to be clear about the choices that we make and take responsibility for the consequences.

So don't be afraid to use the 'no' word; it's more positive than you might realise.

DON'T QUIT

I occasionally start doing a jigsaw on a cosy winter evening, and before long find that it's just too difficult, with too much of the same colour, or there are pieces I can't find, or it's too big, and having started off well, I sometimes abandon it.

Have you ever felt like quitting anything? Ever felt like throwing in the towel? Ever felt fed up to a point of abandon? There are times when it would be easy to give up on yourself, your marriage, your kids, your job, your hopes, your dreams, but today is a day to hold tight, look up, and hang on in there.

Don't quit. It's really not worth it, and it's not your only option.

Several characters in the Bible faced situations where they were ready to quit: Jeremiah, Jonah, Elijah, Job, but then God came and helped them, and they were able to continue, and He can help you too - so don't quit!

Even Jesus, in the days leading up to His death on the cross, in the garden of Gethsemane, prayed to God 'If it is possible, take this cup from me.' Luke 22:42. He then pressed through those feelings and continued in order to complete the task ahead.

Allow perseverance to finish its work in you so that you may be mature and complete in character and hope.

WE KNOW
THAT SUFFERING
PRODUCES
PERSEVERANCE
perseverance,
CHARACTER
AND CHARACTER

hope.
ROMANS 5:4

ENDURING CHANGE

Change can be an exciting and positive adjustment, like moving your furniture around, redecorating the house, or simply buying a new shade of lipstick. An even bigger change would be a new job, marriage, having a new baby, a bereavement or a divorce. Change brings transformation and difference to the way things were.

Sometimes changes are hard to handle and can be painful.

Mark Twain once said "The only people who like change are wet babies!"

Change can be unnerving or unsettling and sometimes we resist change because it's easier to stick with what is familiar.

Have you ever wished that someone you know would change? Have you ever wished you could change? Change your actions, your thoughts, your attitude, your appearance, your outlook, your dreams, your past, your future?

For a change to be lasting, it must come from the inside out. Only God can affect that type of 'heart' change.

So if you need a change and you've tried different things but nothing seems to stick, perhaps it's a change of heart you need.

CREATE IN ME A PURE HEART,

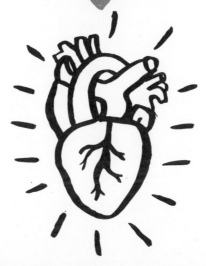

AND RENEW A
STEADFAST SPIRIT
WITHIN ME.
PSALM 51:10-12

FORGIVE AND FORGET

Have you noticed that children are much better at 'forgiving and forgetting' than grown-ups? Do you remember falling out with friends when you were a child, and then the next minute being inseparable again? As we grow up, forgiving takes on a whole new meaning, and becomes a bigger challenge to us as misunderstandings happen, and conflicts come our way.

We think maybe that if we forgive, it justifies what was done to us, making it alright.

Christian author, Stormie Omartian, who went through mistreatment and all sorts of problems as a child and teen, says "Forgiveness doesn't make the other person right, it just makes you free."

Sometimes we carry things, and they become a heavy load, but forgiveness can change things. Real forgiveness isn't just acting; it's saying 'sorry' and 'I forgive you' with our heart. Genuine forgiveness leaves no thoughts of revenge. You know forgiveness is real when you have stopped talking about the incident and recalling it over and over again.

Sincere forgiveness needs God's help. The Lord's prayer teaches us that God forgives us and helps us to forgive others and this prevents us being consumed with bitterness.

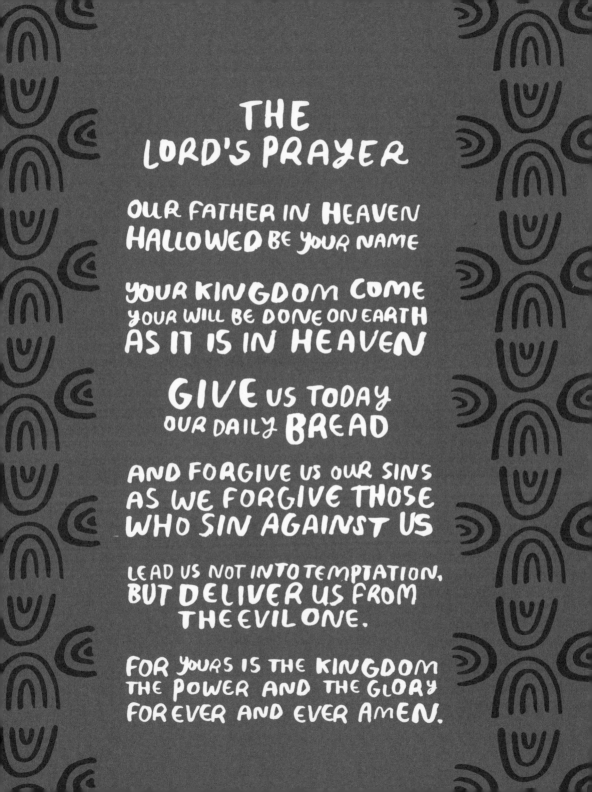

FINE NOT TO BE FINE

How are you today? You may well reply, "Hi Sarah I'm fine thanks." And you might say to me "And how are you?" And I might reply, "Yeah I'm good thanks." But one of us may not be telling the full truth. How often have you said 'fine', and in your head you are thinking 'Actually I'm not fine, but will say 'fine' because that's easier and it's what's expected?'

I've got some good news for you today. It's fine to not be fine. You have permission. You are allowed lows as well as highs, you are allowed to have off days, you are allowed to feel like kicking the cat, and you are allowed to be tired and frustrated. You have permission!

Especially as a mum, there are times things get a bit much and you just don't feel on top of things. Then again there are times when all is well in the world, and that's wonderful too.

I really hope that for you things are under control; that your potty training is going amazingly, that all the bills are up to date, and the people in your world are treating you like a queen. However, for those of you that feel 'not fine', firstly, you are not alone, and secondly, it's fine not to be fine, for a time. This season will pass, as sure as night follows day.

Tomorrow is a new day and you are loved more than you know.

BE ANXIOUS
FOR NOTHING
BUT IN EVERYTHING
BY PRAYER AND &
PETITION, WITH
THANKSGIVING,
PRESENT YOUR
REQUESTS TO GOD.

PHILIPPIANS 4:6

FRIENDS

Most people need them. To have one you have to be one. Each friend is different. The degrees of friendship can differ in closeness, varying from life-long loyal best friends, almost from birth, through to acquaintances; and in general, friends are good for us, as long as we choose the right ones.

The rise of social networking has enabled friends to reconnect and rekindle friendships from school days, or maintain long distance connections across the country and even across oceans.

Think of your list of friends right now. I guess there are those you couldn't imagine doing the journey of life without, and then others who are on the periphery and the margins but who also bring value to your life. Maybe friendships are like concentric circles, like a pebble in the pond effect – the inner circle and the outer circles.

Jesus had really good friends; many hundreds of people followed Him and loved Him, then there were those in an inner circle, commonly known as the twelve disciples, and from those twelve he had three closer friends, Peter, James and John.

Jesus knew the value of true friendship and companionship, and was the perfect friend who loved unconditionally and his friends wanted to be with Him.

Sometimes when it was necessary He spoke to His friends with wisdom, insight and advice; the sort that hits a raw nerve but actually made them think and re-evaluate. Solomon writes in the book of Proverbs 27:6 'precious are the wounds of a friend.'

My friends both far and near mean the world to me and I couldn't imagine life without them! Each one so different and unique, but all adding that something extra special to my life and I'm grateful.

THE ONE WHO HAS FRIENDS
MUST HIMSELF BE FRIENDLY
BUT THERE IS A FRIEND WHO STICKS
CLOSER THAN A BROTHER.

PROVERBS 18:24

GAINING THROUGH LOSS

Have you ever felt a sense of loss? It could be loss of a friendship, loss of a job, loss of finances, loss of security, loss of a relationship, loss of a loved one...the list goes on. Loss isn't easy to deal with.

Loss can really affect you and shake you up, and you wonder how you can move on. Loss can make you feel insecure for a while, and knock your confidence and your identity.

Often in times of loss there is a lot to be gained. We see a new perspective, we care more about others' losses, we learn who really loves and supports us, and we find new ways forward and learn about hope.

Joseph, a great young man in the Bible, famous for his coat of many colours, went through tough challenges as his family turned against him and mistreated him. He was imprisoned and betrayed, but his conclusion was that the things that seemed like they were going to harm him actually turned out for good, and he gained through his losses. Interesting isn't it?

For in the dark cloud of all of our losses, there is a silver lining – with God's help, we gain, we grow stronger, and we can change for the better.

For a little while you
have had to suffer grief
in all kinds of trials.
These have come so that
your faith-of greater
worth than gold which
perishes even refined
by fire- may be proved
genuine and may result
in praise, glory and
honour when Jesus
Christ is revealed.

1 Peter 1:6-7

GRATITUDE

How grateful are you for all that you have in your life? It's so easy sometimes to lose sight of the good things and be sidetracked to dwell on what you haven't got instead of what you have . To be grateful is to be 'warmly appreciative especially of kindness received'.

Do you find it easy to express gratitude? How do you show you are grateful? We might forget to say thank you, and carry on as though that gift or that event or that kindness someone did for us didn't mean very much, when actually it did. If we don't express being grateful how will they know?

Do you write thank you cards? Send thank you texts? Or have you ever written to a shop or restaurant to say that a member of staff excelled when serving you? It can really make a difference. It's easy to be quick to complain, but let's learn to be just as quick to show appreciation.

We love it when people appreciate us, or when gifts we give are appreciated, so let's be the ones who do the appreciating more and more.

The Bible tells us 'in everything give thanks', so today whatever you are doing, look for those things you are grateful for and say your thank yous to the right people.

GIVE THANKS IN ALL CIRCUMSTANCES FOR THIS IS GOD'S WILL FOR YOU IN CHRIST JESUS

1 THESSALONIANS 5:18

HEAT OF THE MOMENT

Have you ever lost your cool in the heat of the moment? Have you ever said things that afterwards you wish you had never said?

There is nothing worse than anger that simmers away inside of you. The chances are that it might explode when you least expect it, and end up causing hurt to those closest to you. Anger is not something to be proud of because it has the potential to do harm. Anger is something to be prayed about, dealt with, and diffused.

Some things wind us up, make us cross, or cause us to 'fly off the handle', but the Bible says 'be angry and sin not'. In other words, being cross isn't the end of the world, but just be on your guard that it doesn't cause you to do or say something you'll regret for a long time.

Deal with it in a healthy way, but don't let it linger, because it will only grow and steal your happiness.

Another piece of advice from the Bible is 'don't let the sun go down on your wrath.' In other words, clear the air, back down and say sorry before the day is out. Holding on to anger isn't conducive to a good night's sleep!

Sort things out as much as you are able to, the sooner the better and don't carry it through to the next day. Tomorrow is a new day.

BE ANGRY AND DO
NOT SIN; DO NOT
LET THE SUN
GO DOWN ON YOUR
ANGER.

EPHESIANS 4:26

HISTORY MAKERS

We all have an ancestry and a family background and I'm sure our families are a bit similar; ordinary people, some odd, some quirky.

Most families are a group of people who stick together through thick and thin; a social cluster of parents and children, possibly living under the same roof but definitely connected to one another by birth, adoption or circumstances. The modern day family is not easy to define, but families are the building blocks of society.

In researching my family tree over the years, I've thought a lot about our family, and the legacy left by those who are no longer with us. There are so many inspirational stories of amazing people who endured, fought, survived and thrived.

We often forget that we are writing history today. One day there will be records about you and I. What sort of legacy are you leaving for the future generations?

Legacy is so different to inheritance. Legacy is what we give, and inheritance is about what we get. Legacy has little to do with finances, and much more about character, example, and the gifts we give to future generations.

So what can we do today to make a difference to the lives of those around us? We can't change the past within our families; history has been made.

We can however change things for the future, with God's help. I'm pretty keen to be a history maker. What about you?

I HAVE SET YOU
AN EXAMPLE
THAT YOU SHOULD
DO AS I HAVE
DONE FOR YOU

JOHN 13:15

HOME

During our time living in Zambia back in the late 1990's, I once visited a very poor widow living in a remote rural area, about an hour from where we lived. She and her children lived in a one roomed mud hut, and her chickens were very much at home there too. I will never forget the day she welcomed us into her home - it was so humbling. There were some very basic blankets on the floor, a hand-made rug on the hardened earth, some pots and pans and very little else; but it was her home. It was her safe place and her refuge. She did all the cooking on an open fire and cauldron outside, and there was no sanitation, and definitely no electricity or running water.

What does the word 'home' mean to you? How does it make you feel? Home is generally a place where a person or a family lives, spends time, where they are comfortable being. Of course the concept of 'home' is much more than a literal dwelling of bricks and mortar, or straw and mud. Home is that feeling of refuge and comfortable safety, and the place you belong, and home is where your heart is. There are lots of places where I feel totally at home, but it's not necessarily where I live.

Neal A. Maxwell says "Good homes are still the best source of good humans," and that is so true, because how things are at home has been known to influence people's behaviour, emotions, and overall well being.

However things are for you at home at the moment behind those closed doors, whatever you are facing, however you feel, whatever you are thinking, hang in there.

It could be that you will bring change to the atmosphere and make your home a place where people want to be.

DO NOT NEGLECT TO SHOW HOSPITALITY TO STRANGERS, FOR BY SO DOING SO SOME PEOPLE HAVE ENTERTAINED ANGELS WITHOUT KNOWING IT.

HEBREWS 13:2

I'M TIRED

Have you ever woken up still feeling tired? Not just tired, but exhausted? This can be quite common when you have a busy life and many demands. Sometimes you get so used to just being permanently worn out, that it becomes -the 'new normal'.

Maybe we need to grasp the difference between sleep and rest. We need to factor into our lives proper rest. Physical rest, which can include sleep, mental rest, where we switch off and enjoy a hobby or take a walk, or play music and rest our busy minds. What about sensory rest? Rest from our phones and laptops and gadgets. Rest our eyes, rest our senses. We need emotional rest - learning to step back from the things that drain us, and not being afraid to say 'no' to that one extra demand. We also need spiritual rest which involves quietly praying, resting and being still.

It's perfectly acceptable to be tired because of our circumstances and the demands of life, that's quite normal, but the time to be concerned is when we are tired of our life. That's different. But even then, there is hope as you are revived and restored in Christ.

Be kind to yourself, accept every offer of help, factor in the necessary rest, have a chat with a trusted friend, and even when you are tired, keep focused on the things that matter most.

Despite exhaustion, we can have strength for the day. Deuteronomy 33:25 says 'As your days, so shall your strength be'. **One day at a time, one step at a time, and one season at a time, there is enough strength for you today and tomorrow.**

JESUS SAID
COME UNTO ME
ALL WHO ARE WEARY
AND I WILL GIVE
YOU REST

MATTHEW 11 v 28

JUDGE NOT

Have you ever made an assessment of someone or something based on what you see, and found out that you were wrong? It's very easy to do, but often things are not always as they seem. We all tend to 'judge a book by its cover', meaning that we determine the worth of something based upon its appearance.

Growing up at home, my Dad was very proud of the fake bunch of black grapes in the fruit bowl. It fooled so many people, especially as we had a beautiful vine in the greenhouse in our garden. I've seen many guests trying to pluck a plastic grape.
The black grapes looked so realistic and they brought a lot of giggles over the years.

In the words of William Shakespeare 'All that glitters is not gold.' Not everything that looks real actually is. Fake goods are deceiving customers every day. They look so genuine, but they are replications of the real thing.

How true it is that we all can misjudge what we see, and come to wrong conclusions.

In the Old Testament, when a new king was to be selected from Jesse's sons, it ended up being the least likely son, David, who was chosen. Not the one who looked the part, was the most handsome or had the greatest credentials, but the one with the right heart.

A man sees what is visible to the eyes but God sees into the heart." 1 Samuel 16:7

LOOK AT THE THINGS

THE LORD DOES NOT

PEOPLE LOOK AT

PEOPLE LOOK AT THE OUTWARD APPEARANCE BUT THE LORD LOOKS AT THE HEART

1 SAMUEL 16:7

KEY TO HAPPINESS

There is a Proverb that says 'He who refreshes others shall himself be refreshed'.

Also we read in Matthew 7:12, 'do unto others as you have them do unto you.' Could this be a key to happiness? Does bringing joy to others make you happy? Do you love buying that perfect gift for someone and seeing their reaction?

It's easy to get caught up in our own happiness and our own needs, and as long as we are alright that's all that really matters.

Maybe that's not the best way to live.

Life takes on a new dimension when you wake up in the morning and consciously think what can I do today that will make a difference for someone else.

What words can I say that will bring comfort? What smile might lift someone out of their sadness? What bunch of flowers will let someone know that I care? What cake can I bake? What help can I give?

Take hold of that key today – it might change your day around.

HE WHO REFRESHES OTHERS SHALL HIMSELF BE REFRESHED

PROVERBS 11:25

LONELINESS

There are times in our lives when we are prone to feeling more lonely than others: After a bereavement, during illness or hospitalisation, when our family lives far away, when our children flee the nest, or just during winter time when we are indoors more.

There is a difference between being alone and being lonely. You can be alone and not be at all lonely. You can have no one else around and yet be so satisfied and content, so enjoying yourself that you do not need or miss anyone else. Or you can be in the middle of a crowd, with people all around you doing many things, and with your heart aching inside of you because of loneliness. Modern city life has been aptly described as, "millions of people being lonesome together."

In today's culture we are taught to become more independent and that admitting we need each other is a sign of weakness. But it's not. We do need each other. God didn't intend for people to be lonely. He intended for us to live, love and share our lives together with others in families, communities, churches and social groups.

The cure for loneliness is not a pill, or a scheme or anything else, but rather a person. And Jesus has created a special place in our hearts that only He can fill.

With Jesus in our life, we are never alone.

GOD SETS THE LONELY IN FAMILIES

PSALM 68:6

LOOKING FORWARD

What do you most look forward to? The weekend? Going on holiday? Getting out of debt? The Christmas season? Losing weight and dropping a dress size? Buying instead of renting a home? An evening with friends? A special celebration? A time when your family is more independent? Better health? A change of direction? That new opportunity on the horizon?

Sometimes we stop dreaming and hoping and looking forward because we've been disappointed in the past and we daren't hope again, or because we're experiencing depression and are too low to see beyond today. Sometimes we stop dreaming because we can't ever see things changing for the better in our life or situation. Maybe we are fearful of what the future might hold. We can't allow ourselves the vulnerability to dream and hope of better days ahead.

We need hope, which is the ability to look forward to the future with confidence and expectation. Hope is closely linked with our faith - the ability to see beyond the here and now, and look forward to a future which is mapped out by God.

He spans the past, present and future, and is willing to lead us and guide us onward and upward. You can safely put your confidence and trust in Him

As the saying goes, 'We don't know what tomorrow holds, but we know who holds tomorrow' and it is for that reason alone we can have hope.

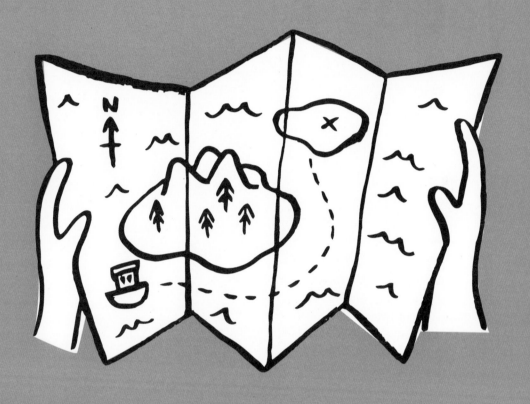

NOW FAITH IS BEING
SURE OF WHAT WE HOPE FOR
AND CERTAIN OF
WHAT WE DO NOT SEE.

HEBREWS 11:1

LOST

Have you ever lost anything? Your all important mobile phone? What about those vital car keys? A letter or document? What about your purse or wallet? Or have you ever been lost anywhere? When you were a child were you ever lost in a supermarket? Lost on a busy beach? Or have you lost a child that you should have been watching closely? You blinked and they wandered off. Have you ever had your name called over a tannoy of a department store so you can be reunited with those who wandered from you or you from them? It's not a nice feeling and it causes us to panic. Do you find that other people in your family expect you to have 'special powers' to locate their lost things in your home too? You are the one who should know where everything is.

What about in our everyday lives? Sometimes you can feel like you have lost your way a little, or lost hope, or lost direction, or even feel like you have lost the plot or lost your mind!

Some may have lost love. 'It is better to have loved and lost than never to have loved at all' said the poet Tennyson, but the reality of that is painful.

In Luke 15, there are three stories of lost things that are found again: a coin, a sheep and a son. The Lost Son in the chapter had 'lost it all', by going his own way and squandering his inheritance, but one day made his way back to his Father and family, and was 'found' again and there was cause for great celebration. The Father in the story represents God and He is wonderful at helping people who have lost 'it' whatever 'it' may be.

He finds us right where we are and rescues us.

I TELL YOU THERE WILL BE

MORE REJOICING

IN HEAVEN

OVER 1 SINNER WHO
REPENTS THAN OVER
99 RIGHTEOUS PERSONS
WHO DO NOT NEED TO
REPENT

LUKE 15:7

MASKS

My children always loved the dressing up box, and often their outfits included a mask, covering their faces, transforming them into the appropriate character. In seconds they were living out the role of someone else, whether it was Spiderman or Snow White.

Do you ever wear a mask? Have you ever worn a mask whether it's your surface smile, the cover of makeup, your clothes, your performance, and your lifestyle?

Why do we wear masks? To look like someone else? To hide our pain? To hide the real us from others? I have worn a mask at different times for a variety of reasons. In the Covid 19 pandemic, mask wearing was necessary for our protection.

Those of us who have done so will know that wearing a mask is extremely draining and dehumanising.

No matter how good our mask or how real our performance is, there is one person who knows exactly what's going on. That is God. He knows you because He created you.

There is no need for masks as He knows exactly what you are hiding, and He wants to help take care of your hidden heartache.

O LORD YOU
HAVE SEARCHED ME
AND KNOW ME.
YOU KNOW WHEN
I SIT AND WHEN I RISE
YOU UNDERSTAND
MY THOUGHTS
FROM AFAR.

PSALM 139:1-2

MEDICINE KISSES

Whenever one of our children experienced the inevitable fall and scrape as they lost their balance, I used to say 'let Mummy kiss you better'. One day, our youngest had the tiniest cut on his hand, and came running to me and said 'Mummy I need a medicine kiss!' It was just so cute.

It made me think that it's not so much the kiss itself, but it's the love behind it that makes it special. Love is like a soothing medicine in order to make things feel better.

What about us adults? We have progressed from grazed knees and bumped heads, but what about our hearts? Often they are wounded and hurt and need the best medicine of all – love.

We all need the love and tenderness of our family, and our friends, this love is like a healing balm. It does us good, it makes things better, it makes us feel special, and it puts a spring in our step.

However, human love, and how it is expressed, is sometimes a bit fickle and unreliable, but God in heaven loves you with an everlasting love.

There is a safety and security in this love that really makes life worth living.

I HAVE LOVED YOU WITH AN EVERLASTING LOVE; I HAVE DRAWN YOU WITH UNFAILING KINDNESS

JEREMIAH 31: 3

MiRACLE

We are all living miracles! A miracle is simply an extraordinary or supernatural event considered as a work of God, and that's exactly who we are, summed up in a nutshell.

I admire people who believe in evolution. It takes a lot of 'faith' to believe that life just 'happened'. It's like saying that my laptop just threw itself together in a factory and all the components just aligned with one another without any help or assistance from anyone.

Knowing there is a Creator God, who gives life, makes complete sense to me. Someone, somewhere designed His creation down to the finest detail. Who thought up the four chambers of the heart? The network of blood vessels around the body? The multiple functions of the liver that keep us alive and healthy? The structure of our skeleton to keep us standing and moving?

And what about the plant and animal world? From the largest whale, to the tiniest insect, and the way that they live in their own habitats and all function differently - it's simply miraculous!

What about the tiniest petal, or largest tree in a tropical forest, each one in the right place and all connected in the ecosystem to bring fruit, flowers and beauty to our world. Every butterfly or ladybird, golden eagle or garden sparrow, each designed and wonderfully made.

So today, thank God for the miracle that you are, and every miracle you see around you today.

In the words of the well known hymn 'We plough the fields and scatter' we sing, 'He only is the Maker of all things near and far...He paints the wayside flower, He lights the evening star...so thank the Lord for all His love.

GENESIS 1:1-3

MONEY MONEY MONEY

Having lived in Zambia for two years, I have seen poverty with my own eyes, and yet, the incredible thing is that some of the happiest people I have ever met have been those with very little worldly possessions.

Does money buy you happiness? Can money buy you friends? Does money guarantee success? Can money buy you health? For sure we can't live without it, and sometimes we wish we had a little bit more, but it's also generally true that the more you have, the more you spend. It's also the case that money matters cause a great deal of stress and sleepless nights. I have a magnet on my fridge that says 'the best things in life are not things.' I like that. Also similarly, the best things in life are free.

There is more to life than what you own or don't own, and what you owe or don't owe. Regardless of our financial circumstances, our status or our bank balance, we can know riches and treasures of a different sort as a result of our faith in Jesus. And because of this living hope in Christ, we have an inheritance that can never perish, spoil or fade.

Jesus said in Luke's gospel 'Be on your guard against all kinds of greed; life does not consist in an abundance of possessions.'

A MAN'S LIFE DOES NOT CONSIST IN THE ABUNDANCE OF HIS POSSESSIONS

LUKE 12:15

NATIVITY

I'm sure you can remember when you were younger getting dressed up as angels or shepherds, and even hitting the big time by being chosen to be Mary or Joseph or Gabriel. Wow – what an honour!

At our community charity shop one Autumn, someone handed in a shoe box, and as we opened it, inside was the cutest knitted nativity set you have ever seen. It included the full cast of characters and even the sheep! The thing that was so adorable though, was the fact that there was a spare Baby Jesus. He was so tiny, that whoever knitted it must have thought that it's just too tempting for kids to pick up, put him in their pocket and do a runner, so she did a spare.

That really made me think – it's the time of year where Jesus can so easily be misplaced or lost in all the hustle and bustle, the spending, the planning, gift ordering and food shopping, that He gets overlooked and can so easily be taken out of the equation.

It's spelt C-H-R-I-S-T-M-A-S, if you take Christ out of it, you have nothing.

Keep things in perspective this Christmas, keep Jesus central, and celebrate Him, and then things take on a new meaning.

DO NOT BE AFRAID.
I BRING YOU GOOD NEWS
THAT WILL CAUSE GREAT
JOY FOR ALL THE PEOPLE.
TODAY, IN THE TOWN OF
DAVID A SAVIOUR
HAS BEEN BORN TO YOU;
HE IS THE MESSIAH,
THE LORD.

LUKE 2:10-11

NEW YEAR NEW YOU

Once the New Year's Eve celebrations are out of the way, and the Christmas decorations are packed away, the reality of the year ahead can fill some of us with apprehension. Maybe stepping into the unknown frightens you – or maybe a new year excites you, with fresh adventures.

What challenges do we face in the New Year? Maybe, you're thinking I didn't achieve a great deal last year. However, if you sit down and think about it, you may have moved house, changed jobs, given birth, got married, learnt a new skill, travelled somewhere new, done some training, or changed something significant in your life, all of which are great achievements!

New Year's resolutions - do you make any? Do you stick to them? Do you have a list of everything you want to change? Whether it's a diet, getting a new job, changing the way you see yourself, adjusting your life - goals and dreams.

Perhaps we all would like some things to change this year.

Change for the better and the greatest change of all, is the one that happens inside us.

Only God can bring true and lasting change, and it starts in our hearts and minds. New Year and a new you, with change from the inside out.

DO NOT CONFORM TO THE PATTERN OF THIS WORLD BUT BE TRANSFORMED BY THE RENEWING OF YOUR MIND.

ROMANS 12:2

ONE LIFE

Time seems to be going faster than ever.

When I was a child, I remember the Summer holidays seemed to be endless, as we played outside all day long, and a full day at school seemed to last hour upon hour. And yet it's still the same seven days a week, twenty four hours a day, sixty minutes an hour now, as it was then.

You'll never get time back again so what you do with your time today is important.

Where you invest your time matters, and your time input into the lives of children, young people, and those in your world is totally precious. You will never get this time back again, so enjoy it and value it.

The Bible teaches us about not wasting time on worrying about what may never happen, but instead live fully today, maximise your time by using it wisely.

Not so much counting the hours, but making the hours count.

BUT SEEK FIRST HIS KINGDOM AND HIS RIGHTEOUSNESS, AND ALL THESE THINGS WILL BE GIVEN TO YOU AS WELL. THEREFORE DO NOT WORRY ABOUT TOMORROW FOR EACH DAY HAS ENOUGH TROUBLE OF ITS OWN.

MATTHEW 6:33-34

PEACE!

Have you ever said to yourself 'I need some peace!?'

You may not get enough peace. Perhaps by the time that blanket of peace falls on the home in the late evening you are too exhausted to fully appreciate and enjoy it. Does that sound familiar?

What if peace isn't to do with your circumstances or your surroundings or the seeming chaos sometimes in our busy homes, but more to do with your heart?

Could it be that in the middle of the storm, you can still have peace in your heart?

Are you good at making peace by reconciling? That is such a wonderful quality to possess if you are able to do that, it shows great character.

Are you at peace? The Bible says that Jesus gives peace, not like the world gives, it can't be bought or earned, just received, like a gift.

So if you are making peace, keeping the peace, or needing a bit of peace remember the most important thing is to BE at peace.

PEACE
I LEAVE WITH YOU;
MY PEACE I GIVE
YOU. I DO NOT
GIVE TO YOU AS THE
WORLD GIVES.
DO NOT LET YOUR
HEARTS BE TROUBLED
AND DO NOT BE AFRAID.

JOHN 14:27

PERFECTION

Have you noticed that things in your life are not as perfect as you would like them to be?

You haven't got a perfect body (because we all want to change something), perfect finances, perfect marriages, and definitely not perfect children. Even though others may look at you and think things seem perfect, you know they are far from it.

So do we keep striving for perfectionism and make ourselves stressed with our efforts, or do we try a different approach?

Maybe it's time to change the focus of our gaze on the things that are faulty in our eyes, and the demands we put on others and ourselves for things to be better than they are. Instead we can look at everything that is good, and celebrate it.

We can never be perfect, because we live in an imperfect world, so just be you and stop striving.

There is only one person who is perfect in every way and that is Jesus, God's son.

He is perfect and thankfully He loves imperfect people like us.

LET
US FIX
OUR EYES
ON JESUS
THE PIONEER
AND PERFECTER
OF OUR FAITH

HEBREWS 12:2

PIGGY IN THE MIDDLE

Did you ever play that game as a child? Two players pass the ball to one another with a third person in the middle trying to intercept it.

That term 'piggy in the middle' can also refer to someone in between two other parties, or someone caught between two sides of a dispute. Have you ever been in the middle of a 'situation'? It can be a very awkward and uncomfortable place to be.

However, being in the middle is also a great place to be. Think of all the ambassadors in the world, representing us in another country. Think of the people who stand in the gap and speak up and resolve issues for those who can't defend themselves.

We will often find ourselves in the middle, but we can use that position to bring change and resolution. You are an arbitrator, an ambassador, and intermediary. After all they are not just titles for politicians – they can describe you and I.

If you resolve a small conflict between two children who keenly want the same toy, you are a wonderful arbitrator. If you get two friends to talk again, after months of silence, you are a reconciler. If you speak on behalf of those who don't have a voice, you are an ambassador.

Next time you feel like you're caught in the middle, see it as an opportunity to make a difference between two parties, just as Jesus did for us as He bridged the gap between God and man.

FOR THERE IS ONE GOD
AND ONE MEDIATOR
BETWEEN GOD & MANKIND
THE MAN, CHRIST JESUS

1 TIMOTHY 2:5

PLATE SPINNING

Have you ever been to the circus? Or seen a variety show on television and watched the skilful plate-spinner?

Do you ever feel like you're spinning plates?

If you watch a professional plate spinner, you'll see they apply just enough energy to each plate so that each of them maintain momentum and stay balanced until they come back to give another spin.

What a challenge! To be able to apply enough energy to each responsibility, project, friend, family member, hobby so that you maintain some sort of balance. What a job! That can be exhausting especially if you are doing it alone.

If you successfully learn to spin one plate really well, you can spin many. It takes a great deal of skill, coordination, balance, timing, vision and concentration but that's just what YOU do day in, day out.

You are doing more with your life than you think, so today, be encouraged, you are a highly skilled plate spinner. Well done!

Read about an amazing multitasking woman in Proverbs 31vs10-31.

SHE SETS ABOUT HER WORK VIGOROUSLY; HER ARMS ARE STRONG FOR HER TASKS. HONOUR HER FOR ALL THAT HER HANDS HAVE DONE, AND LET HER WORKS BRING HER PRAISE AT THE CITY GATE.

PROVERBS 31

PRESSURE

Not all pressure is bad – we need a certain amount of blood pressure to be alive, we need atmospheric pressure, and pressure washers are certainly a good invention! What none of us need or like is excess pressure, the sort that causes stress that becomes unmanageable.

What sort of pressure do you sometimes feel? Peer pressure? Financial pressure? Pressure within your family and relationships? Pressure of problems that you think no one understands? Do you ever feel squeezed? Do you ever feel weighed down?

Paul in the book of Acts writes that he felt 'hard pressed, but not crushed'. That's interesting, maybe because he asked for God's help there was some relief to the pressure, or maybe he realised that courage and patience are needed for these times, or maybe he also realised that pressurised times don't last forever. Whatever his reasoning and insight, there was a certain hope for the pressure he faced.

What about you? What's the answer? When I was young my Mum had a pressure cooker and when using it, every now and again she would have to release the pressure by lifting a nozzle and a big squirt of high pressured steam would come out. What's your relief valve when the pressure gets too much? How do you let off steam? Is that just a temporary solution? How can we handle pressure healthily?

Find what works for you and take time to bring the stress levels down again.

FOR OUR LIGHT AND MOMENTARY TROUBLES ARE ACHIEVING FOR US AN ETERNAL GLORY THAT FAR OUTWEIGHS THEM ALL. SO WE FIX OUR EYES NOT ON WHAT IS SEEN BUT ON WHAT IS UNSEEN. SINCE WHAT IS SEEN IS TEMPORARY.

2 CORINTHIANS 4:17-18

QUIET TIME

Picture the scene - you are lying on a tropical beach, with the sun's rays pouring down on you, and all you can hear is the gentle lapping of the waves on the shore. Or, you are sitting in a sunny conservatory with a coffee and a good book. The home is quiet, it's just you... and breathe!

For those of us who live with a family, quiet moments can be rare. Often, from the moment you wake, until you place your head on the pillow again, there are demands, and there is noise!

'Silence is golden' the saying goes, and I must admit, the older I get, the more I value quietness and space. I love sitting in my car, with a hot drink in a flask, and enjoy the contained quietness as I look at a beautiful scene.

In the quietness, we can think clearly, and other voices are far away. We can find soothing moments, healing, prayerful moments that can't be found in the noise.

There are times when I need my eighties tunes or gospel choir music blasting, and there are times when I equally need to sit still, and sit quietly. Both are replenishing in their own way.

Isaiah 30:15 says 'In quietness and confidence is your strength' and I'm beginning to realise how invaluable this is.

Rest is good. Stillness is good. Quietness is good.

COME WITH ME
BY YOURSELVES
TO A QUIET PLACE
AND GET SOME REST

MARK 6:31

REGRETS

Do you have any regrets in life? Have you ever said or thought 'if only.' We have all made decisions and experienced things we would like to change when we look back on our lives.

Regret involves wishing we could have said or done something differently.

There are two types of regrets; the first, a regret of inaction, for something we could have done but didn't e.g. not getting a degree because we chose to do something else. The second, a regret of action, for something we did do but wish we hadn't. These regrets can cause us heartache and pain – from spending money we shouldn't have, to not making more effort with a friendship or relationship.

The reality is that we all have 'what ifs', but we need to get to the place where we forget what we didn't do and accept what we did, even if it means facing the circumstances or learning from them.

We can choose to make the best of what we've got now. Some of those decisions have made you who you are today, both the good and the not so good.

If you are struggling with regret, try to realise that nothing is gained by dwelling on the past, and that God has the ability to turn things around for good if we ask Him to.

AND WE KNOW
THAT IN ALL THINGS
GOD WORKS FOR THE
GOOD OF THOSE WHO
LOVE HIM, WHO
HAVE BEEN CALLED
ACCORDING TO HIS
PURPOSE

ROMANS 8V28

SEASONS

We are creatures of seasons and times especially us wonderful females – we are creatures of seasons and cycles!

There are patterns and cycles in our lives and we shouldn't be surprised about that because God created the world with times and seasons.

After all, He designed day and night, light and dark, Spring, Summer, Autumn, and Winter.

We need to understand that there are reasons for seasons, and that certain things happen at certain times in our lives. It is so releasing to simply accept your season, and the contentment that accompanies that is priceless.

We clear out our wardrobes, we spring clean, we sort out our homes to prepare for a season change and so as sure as night follows day, and day follows night, life changes and seasons change.

Always be ready for a change of season. Just as we see in nature, in the Autumn, dead leaves fall, to make way for new things, one season makes way for another.

THERE IS A TIME
FOR EVERYTHING
AND A SEASON
FOR EVERY ACTIVITY
UNDER HEAVEN

ECCLESIASTES 3:1

SHARE

It's rather hilarious watching young children play together, and seeing them grasp the principle of 'sharing' or not fully comprehending it, whatever the case might be. When they have their heart set on a particular toy or activity and then a grown up tells them they need to share it, that's challenging!

There is something inherent in our humanity to say 'It's mine!' We have to help children to learn the principle of sharing, and often need to be reminded of it ourselves.

What a vital lesson it is that will help us through life. We could call it 'give and take', making sacrifices for others and sharing what we have. Sometimes it's not easy to compromise or put your own needs to one side and sacrifice for others, but it's a beautiful way to live, with many rewards.

The greatest blessing in life is being able to share our lives with others in families, communities, friendships, social groups, churches and organisations. Sharing our resources, our skills, our gifts, our love, our encouragement and simply sharing the heart of who we are with others. How wonderful it is to share support and care, wisdom, good advice and reliable insight with others, and receive from others in the same way.

Life is better when we share the journey with wonderful companions.

A FRIEND LOVES
AT ALL TIMES,
AND A BROTHER
IS BORN FOR
ADVERSITY.

PROVERBS 17:17

SMALL THINGS

Small is sometimes equated to being insignificant, trivial, or unimportant. Small is not inferior. You might feel small sometimes, overlooked or even invisible, but that is not true.

What about small people, the children in our world. They are so massively important, and your job in loving them and nurturing them is so incredible.

Once when the disciples were trying to get the children out of the way (probably for the usual reasons that we love to get them off to bed, being too noisy, grumpy and squabbling) Jesus said 'Let the children come to me'. He has an eye for small things and small people and He loves them.

Right through the Bible we see small things being so very important – from a small stone that killed the giant Goliath, to two small fish and five small loaves that fed 5000 people. Zaccheaus was a small man who climbed a sycamore tree to get to see Jesus, and he was certainly seen by Him.

Jesus also speaks in parables about the importance of small seeds and the way they grow into great trees, flourishing, and giving support to all the birds in the garden.

Small is significant!

THEN JESUS ASKED 'WHAT IS THE KINGDOM OF GOD LIKE? WHAT SHALL I COMPARE IT TO?'

IT IS LIKE A MUSTARD SEED, WHICH A MAN TOOK AND PLANTED IN HIS GARDEN. IT GREW & BECAME A TREE, AND THE BIRDS PERCHED IN ITS BRANCHES

LUKE 13:18-19

SORRY

It's a relatively small word, but one with huge implications. It has the ability to change things, put things right and restore broken relationships of all sorts.

Children, as well as grown-ups, often have situations they need to apologise for. We encourage children to make up with a friend or a sibling and say sorry. It's a good way to resolve issues and deal with matters so no lasting damage is done.

What about in our lives? How often do you use that 'sorry' word? Does it come easily or are you often prone to digging your heels in and not backing down? Do you stubbornly resist sometimes?

To be genuinely sorry is very powerful, regardless of how minor or major the situation might be. Sorry can bring lasting change, mend a broken heart, and even bring lasting peace. When it's on the tip of your tongue, and you struggle to say the word, just realise how liberating it is and what positive change it can bring.

If someone says a heartfelt sorry to you, accept that gift which will have needed their courage, and move on. It's not always easy to say, but those five letters can certainly bring healing and begin to resolve situations for us.

BEAR WITH EACH
OTHER AND FORGIVE
ONE ANOTHER IF ANY
OF YOU HAS A GRIEVANCE
AGAINST SOMEONE.
FORGIVE AS THE LORD
FORGAVE YOU.
AND OVER ALL THESE
VIRTUES PUT ON LOVE,
WHICH BINDS THEM
ALL TOGETHER IN
PERFECT UNITY.

COLOSSIANS 3:13-14

SPRING CLEANING

Apparently September is now officially spring cleaning month, evidenced by a huge surge in cleaning products being purchased, higher than any other time of the year.

It seems that once summer visitors have left us, and children start school again, with their trail of sand in every room, many of us get our houses cleaned and sorted.

A good sort out gives us a great feeling, whether you spring clean your handbag, your car, or clean out your purse or wallet of all those old receipts.

What about a different type of spring cleaning? One that involves our hearts? Just like my house becomes full of unnecessary dust, dirt, sand and a heap of other things, so my heart can get a bit clogged up with stuff that's not so helpful. The dirty smear of a grudge, the stain of a hurtful comment, the grime of regret, it could be anything, the list is endless.

I regularly ask God to give me a heart clean and I feel so much better for it. I know that on our life's journey we will face many twists and turns, but God can make our hearts clean if we ask.

Is it spring cleaning time for you?

SEARCH ME, GOD
AND KNOW
MY HEART;
TEST ME AND KNOW
MY ANXIOUS
THOUGHTS.
SEE IF THERE IS
ANY OFFENSIVE WAY
IN ME, AND LEAD
ME IN THE WAY
EVERLASTING

PSALM 139 :23-24

STICKING TOGETHER

How many of you know that falling in love was the easy bit?! When your eyes met across the crowded room, or when you were swept off your feet at school with that crush, or when that friend introduced you, or you were at that event and they made their way to chat with you- that was just the beginning!

And now years later, how are things going? All of us have the responsibility of maintaining great relationships and not becoming one of those statistics of failing marriages. There is far too much to lose. So how do we keep the fire glowing?

Never stop dating – set some time aside for both of you. Remember it is 'give and take' – if you invest 'in' you will benefit 'from.'

'I am sorry', 'I was wrong', 'Forgive me' are all powerful phrases and can quickly halt an argument that is getting out of control.

Relationships take great effort – don't become complacent. Remember that love is a decision as well as a feeling. Love is a verb - it's a choice. It needs action. It's an ongoing promise to a person.

If you said your vows sincerely, you can always ask for God's help.

Stick together through thick and thin and it will be worth it.

HIS MOUTH IS
SWEETNESS ITSELF;
HE IS ALTOGETHER
LOVELY.
THIS IS MY LOVER
THIS IS MY FRIEND.

SONG OF SONGS 5:16

THE POWER OF LOVE

Have you noticed that those we love the most have flaws and weaknesses? When you love someone, part of the way your love is expressed is by being able to overlook their failings, or at least cover them over with love. Love enables you to choose not to ponder over things that would get between you. Love and forgiveness work hand in hand in any relationship.

This passage from 1 Corinthians 13:4-7 is often read at weddings and it's a great description of what love is.

Love is patient, love is kind. It does not envy, it does not boast, it is not proud. It is not rude, it is not self-seeking, it is not easily angered, it keeps no record of wrongs. Love always protects, always trusts, always hopes, always perseveres.

What is love to you? How do you define it? We say I love ice-cream, I love coffee, and I love my family in the same sentence but are they all the same sort of love?

How does being loved make you feel?

Love is such a powerful emotion, and can change things for the people that you do life with. Love works wonders.

Love is like a medicine - it's so healing and comforting and reassuring, and it's something we all need.

LOVE IS PATIENT
LOVE IS KIND.
IT DOES NOT ENVY
IT DOES NOT BOAST.
IT IS NOT RUDE,
IT IS NOT SELF-SEEKING,
IT IS NOT EASILY ANGERED,

IT KEEPS NO RECORD
OF WRONGS.

1 CORINTHIANS 13:4–7

UNDERVALUED

What are you worth? That's a question to think about. If we were to melt you down and remove all the particles from you like magnesium, phosphorus, fat, iron, calcium, salt and sell it, scientists say you would have a certain price tag, and of course this would increase if you had a gold filling or two.

Our sense of worth is often linked to what we do, if we are needed, and the value others place on us. If we think that we aren't doing anything with our lives of any significance, it affects our feelings of self worth and we can feel undervalued.

The most basic need all of us have is a sense of personal worth brought by security and significance. Security means being loved and accepted just for who I am, regardless of what I do. Significance means having meaning or purpose in my life. It's about knowing that we are good at what we do.

Sometimes in childhood, in our formative years, unhealthy self-worth is formed in us, and this can often make it hard to love ourselves and love others. We may feel inferiority, and even be crippled by it, but just remember that our true worth is who we truly are, and not what we do.

Our basic value is not about what we do, it's about who we are.

YOUR EYES SAW MY UNFORMED BODY. ALL THE DAYS ORDAINED FOR ME WERE WRITTEN IN YOUR BOOK BEFORE ONE OF THEM CAME TO BE. HOW PRECIOUS TO ME ARE YOUR THOUGHTS GOD! HOW VAST IS THE SUM OF THEM!

PSALM 139:16-17

VALLEYS

My homeland of Wales is famous for its many hills and valleys that fill the landscape.

Sometimes they are steep sided, with deep and dark gorges, and sometimes they are broad fertile plains, often with a river running through, but a valley always leads you somewhere, and most times to the sea.

Some valleys are notoriously a depressed low lying area, or a wet marshland. Both places where you could get bogged down!

Do you feel in a dip at the moment? It could be that you feel in a valley of some sort today.

Psalm 23 is one of the most famous Psalms in the Bible and it says 'Though I walk through the valley of the shadow of death, I will fear no evil: for You are with me; Your rod and Your staff they comfort me'.

It talks about walking **through** the valley – that's interesting. It really is a passing through place. There is a beginning and an end to it and valleys generally lead to significant places.

Whatever your valley is called today, hold tight, do not fear, you are just passing through.

WHO AM I?

You may know your name and your National Insurance number, but do you sometimes wonder who you really are?

When you were younger you may have been known as somebody's sister or brother, daughter or son, then someone's partner or spouse, and now along the way you have kind of lost who you are - your identity.

We hear a lot today about identity theft and identity fraud. It's so good to have a healthy identity because that helps us to feel a great sense of worth and enables us to live life well.

So who or what do you allow to shape your identity and worth?

We do. We formulate opinions of ourselves based sometimes on what the mirror says or what circumstances say, but sometimes that opinion can't be trusted.

Others do. Your opinion of me and your encouragement and love for me gives me such a great identity and sense of value. But what about when relationships turn sour?

God does. My opinion and your opinion aren't always right, but what God says is right and true. He clearly says in the Bible that YOU stand out from the crowd and He thinks you are amazing.

So who are you going to listen to?

BUT YOU ARE
A CHOSEN PEOPLE
A ROYAL PRIESTHOOD
A HOLY NATION
GOD'S SPECIAL
POSSESSION
THAT YOU MAY DECLARE
THE PRAISE OF HIM
WHO CALLED YOU OUT
OF DARKNESS INTO HIS
WONDERFUL LIGHT.

1 PETER 2 V9

WORDS

Apparently, women talk up to three times more than men. It is also said that women also talk more quickly, devote more brain power to chatting and even get a buzz out of hearing their own voices!

Someone has even said that "Women use twice as many words as men because they have to repeat everything they say!" That made me smile.

Words are powerful, because with our words we can bring a lot of comfort and love, and also with our words we can do lasting damage.

Think of lies, gossip, slander – who likes being on the receiving end of those sorts of words?

Think about encouraging, complimentary, helpful, kind, sincere words - now they really do make a difference!

If only we could filter the words that come out of our mouths. Sometimes things are out before we know it.

Who of us can say that we have never spoken before thinking, and wished we could have taken the words back.

As words come to the tip of your tongue, ask yourself firstly is it true? Is it kind? And then think, is it necessary to say it?

ALTHOUGH THEY ARE SO
LARGE AND ARE DRIVEN
BY STRONG WINDS, THEY
ARE STEERED BY A VERY
SMALL RUDDER ~~~
LIKEWISE THE TONGUE IS A
SMALL PART OF THE BODY
BUT MAKES GREAT BOASTS.

JAMES 3: 4-5

X − + ÷

Helping our children with their maths homework when they were at school made me wish I had paid more attention in class. However, maths seemed a lot less complex then. It was adding, subtracting, division and multiplication.

Let's do a simple maths lesson together.

ADD What are you adding to your life these days? What are you gaining? What's enhancing you and making you happy? Material things? Patience? More love? What really matters to you?

SUBTRACT What could you do with getting rid of? What could you give away? When did you last declutter? What about getting rid of an attitude? What can you get rid of that isn't doing you any good?

DIVISION In this day and age we see loads of division between couples, families, even friends. It's so easy to let things come between us – think about it and get rid of the wedge. It's not worth it, because life is for loving and living.

MULTIPLICATION Did you know that even the simplest kind thing you do for others is multiplied? There was a little child in the bible who brought to Jesus five loaves and two fish and it ended up feeding thousands.

Our lives have an effect whether good or bad, we can choose.

Multiply love, care, and compassion, let it loose in your life and the sky's the limit.

YOU ARE UNIQUE!

We are all different.

All shapes and sizes, from different backgrounds and childhoods, with different genetic make-up, different fingerprints, different eye construction, and different personalities.

We are all so very unique and special.

After talking at a school assembly on one occasion, a little boy asked me why I had 'one and a half arms'. It's a good question. I was tempted to ask him in return why he had such an array of freckles!

Psalm 139 says that we were 'knit together in our mother's womb'.

There is no-one quite like you and no-one quite like me and even the very hairs of your head are all numbered.

Anything with such detail just had to be made by someone. That someone was God. Do you fancy the idea that you evolved from amoeba? Or that you were designed and created by an awesome God? I know which I prefer.

Thank you God for making us so wonderfully complex. It is amazing to think about. Your workmanship is marvellous—and how well I know it.

FOR YOU CREATED MY INMOST BEING YOU KNIT ME TOGETHER IN MY MOTHER'S WOMB.

PSALM 139:13

ZAMBIA GIFT

Some years ago, I was in our home on the missionary base in Zambia, and the door knocked. Standing before me was a barefoot older lady, holding something wrapped in a piece of cloth. Handing this gift to me, I discovered to my surprise, that it was a new-born baby!

The Grandmother before me had walked for several hours to where the missionaries lived, in the hope that someone could help. Her daughter had given birth in the morning and died in the process of childbirth.

I received this precious bundle into my arms, and the grandmother left. I took my 'gift' back indoors - speechless. Joshua, our eldest son was a year and a half old at the time, and although we wanted another baby, this wasn't quite what I had in mind. I opened the dirty cloth, to find the most adorable baby boy, unwashed, but irresistible. He devoured a bottle of milk and I washed and dressed him and named him Samuel. As I sat there cuddling him Glen arrived home for his lunch break from the mission farm, and was shocked to say the least!

Samuel became one of the first children to be welcomed into the brand new Jabulani Children's Village run by our Danish friends and today is a fine young man, who completed his education, and was reunited with his extended family in Zambia.

I'll never forget that day as long as I live. It changed me, giving me more compassion for people who are helpless.

Can you think of significant, turning point days like that? Days that have shaped you and stayed in your long term memory? Give thanks for that day and the way in which it has changed you for the better.

HE TENDS HIS FLOCK
LIKE A SHEPHERD:
HE GATHERS THE LAMBS
IN HIS ARMS AND
CARRIES THEM CLOSE
TO HIS HEART HE GENTLY
LEADS THOSE THAT
HAVE YOUNG.

ISAIAH 40:11

ABOUT THE AUTHOR
Sarah Chaplin

Sarah is a wife, mother, speaker, leader, author, and a hospital chaplain. Born in Wales, now living in Porthleven, Cornwall, Sarah is married to Glen and they have four children and a son-in-law.

Sarah regularly speaks and tells her story at events and conferences around the UK, and further afield, and loves to communicate the truth of God's word in an inspirational, relevant and practical way.

It is her life's mission to communicate truth wherever she goes. In recent times, she has established 'Truth Told' - a digital presence, with a website **www.truthtold.org.uk** and an inspiring Facebook page with video blogs.

She also published 'Truth Told in Covid Times' in 2020, a small, uplifting and encouraging book of hope.

ABOUT THE ILLUSTRATOR
Melanie Chadwick

Mel is a full-time freelance illustrator, designer and self-confessed sketchoholic.

She loves exploring and drawing and spending time outside in nature and by the sea. She graduated with a degree in Fine Art over 20 years ago and has worked on a variety of creative projects and commissions with clients based in the UK, USA and further afield.

Her illustration work has been published on greeting cards, calendars, gift wrap as well as in recipe books and magazines.

Brought up in Wales, she now lives on the Lizard Peninsula, Cornwall with her husband Tony, who leads a small Christian fellowship, and enjoys running art workshops and sketch walks around the area.

To view more of her work visit **www.melaniechadwick.com**

Thanks for reading our book, we would love to receive your feedback and review. You can connect with us through our Pearls for the Girls facebook page or email via our websites.

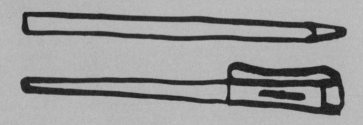